The War in the Gulf

A Diary in Poetry

·TAMAR SEGAL·

First published in 1991 by

WOODFIELD PUBLISHING
Woodfield House, Arundel Road, Fontwell,
West Sussex BN18 0SD, England.

British Library Cataloguing in Publication Data

Tamar Segal
  The war in the gulf: a diary in poetry.
  I. Title.

ISBN 1-873203-06-3

Contents

Foreword

"It is all too easy to forget the tension and real anxiety of the months leading up to the opening of the 'Desert Storm'. Your poems will serve as a reminder of our doubts, fears and concerns during that period."

Air Chief Marshall Sir Thomas Kennedy, GCB AFC DL

"… The range of issues with which you deal is quite comprehensive. In your *Faith and Hope* poem you lead up to a climax which says that you hope the world will be restored to an order that is just and right. I echo that wholeheartedly."

Lord Jakobovits, Chief Rabbi

Introduction

The United Nations enhanced its status by determinedly challenging aggression. Across the world people prayed for a peaceful solution. But when the aggressor confused an earnest desire for peace as weakness, war became inevitable. Although the scene of battle was far away, each action became an integral part of our lives.

Here in Britain all political parties united in a rare way, in support of the forces, and everyone prayed for a speedy peace with a minimum of casualties.

In this diary I share with you the hopes, the fears, the sorrows, the horrors, the relief; and the admiration for those men and women who faced such trials on behalf of us all.

The events were for me all the more poignant, because during the Second World War my husband served with the 4th Armoured Brigade and was blown off the top of an Armoured Command Vehicle when it ran across a mine. Fortunately he recovered after a short period in hospital. During this time I was in England nursing wounded members of the Forces who were flown over from the front.

Throughout the current period of hostilities in the Gulf I felt compelled to write what is known as my Action Poetry to record the unfolding events. By this means, through the years, I have found that I am able to reach out and convey comfort and support to people, including many who usually shut out poetry from their lives.

Some of these verses have been shared with listeners through radio stations in this country and via the Voice of America. It was a privilege to receive responses that I cherish from Her Majesty The Queen, the President of Israel and the Ambassador of the USA.

Gulf charities will receive all royalties from this publication. Hopefully this will play a part in commemorating a significant stand against aggression, will bring some comfort to those who are bereaved, and will strengthen our determination to maintain humanitarian input in that troubled area.

Tamar Segal, May 1990

Tamar Segal

During an official visit to Ravenswood Village for people with severe, profound and multiple disabilities, the Princess Royal remarked to Tamar Segal, the Principal's wife, "If you marry a missionary you must be a missionary's wife." (1972). It was only after 40 years of married life, when Professor Segal retired, that Tamar Segal was again able to concentrate on her own writing career. Nevertheless, her first volume, the *Poetry of Ravenswood*, was about the way of life she had shared with her husband and the Village and was used to assist in raising funds.

She has been interviewed on television, radio and by the press as a result of what the *Independent* was to call her "Action Poetry". Much of her creative energy has been devoted to traumatic events of recent years. In the foyer of the Grand Hotel, Brighton hangs her poem commemorating the terrorist bombing. Margaret Thatcher wrote of it: "You really have caught the spirit of the day". Soho Fire Station contains her poem dedicated to the courageous fireman who died in the Kings Cross Underground Station tragedy; and her poem on the *Marchioness* tragedy is framed on three London piers. She has always seen her work as dedicated to the heroism of both survivors and those who die – the Rt Hon Neil Kinnock commented: "Those who lost their loved ones on the *Marchioness* will always have a deep sense of grief, however I am sure that your words will bring them tremendous comfort."

Her poems on religious themes have stressed the human qualities that are shared by all the great religions and have been published by a variety of journals as well as receiving acknowledgement from the Church of Scotland, Lambeth Palace and different Jewish religious organisations. A poem *We Are All on Trial* was circulated to members of the All Party Parliamentary War Crimes Group. Her most moving experience was ending the "Remembering the Future" gathering of Holocaust survivors at the Sternberg Centre.

Not all Tamar's poems have been on tragic themes. BBC's *Grandstand* commented on the 'strong start' her poem Special Olympics gave their programme, whilst members of the Royal Family, sportsmen (including Paul Gascoigne), musicians (including Sir Charles Groves and a range of orchestras at Kenwood), conferences, family and friends have enjoyed receiving her poems on happier occasions. She is always ready to help charities who approach her for "verse-aid" and a recent poem on the Channel Tunnel will shortly be on view in their Exhibition Hall.

Nevertheless, she mainly chronicles events of impact - and Nurse Daphne Parish, for example, is one of several brave survivors who have written to say: "I appreciate your beautiful poetry and the thoughts that go with them". It is certainly the thought, expressed in poetic form, that matters most to Tamar Segal. Whilst the local press have called her "the People's Poet", her family describe her as "the verse laureate". They consider she has found a way to bring support to people who have gone through major experiences. She herself enjoys the term "action poetry".

It is not surprising that events of this kind should matter to her as Tamar Segal was evacuated from blitzed London after her home was destroyed. She spent the war years as a Red Cross nurse in a hospital where wounded members of both the British services and enemy forces were treated.

Tamar Segal has a daughter Valerie, a son Alan, a son-in-law Michael, and two teenage grand-children Marek and Marsha.

The Nations United

There can be no turning back
no turning the other cheek
to Saddam Hussein
that would be seen
as ineffectual and weak
and then his lethal weapons
would be free to strike a blow
at any neighbouring country
to which he would choose to go.

There should have been a check
on the armaments supplied
no country which has failed in this
can blame the other side.

Now
sooner
rather than later
before
there can be an even more
destructive war
the forces of many nations
are gathering to meet
and with determination
to defeat any offensive
that can now take place
with such grave consequences
for the entire human race.

The cold war now is over
the world can now unite
to halt any ruthless aggressor
for it's not just for oil we fight.

In Question

The Geneva Convention
was agreed
by representatives
of every creed
is it holy
to ignore
such rules as there are
in the conduct of war?
By their deeds
they have made it clear
who the infidels are here.

Oh Israel

O Israel
hear our prayers
Hear O Israel
hear our pleas
for the Promised Land
that welcomes refugees
from the whole world's anti-semitic disease
on you we depend
to defend
what has been built
with joy and pain
may your wisdom humanity and courage ensure
that the blessed State of Israel
remains secure
and we
will listen to your prayers
listen to your pleas
and together find the way to ease
the struggles that we must face
showing our humanity
for the entire human race.

The Longest Mile

The longest mile is now in sight
while armed forces
with their lethal might
are poised in the shifting sand
alert
their weapons skillfully manned
Brinkmanship has run its perilous
course
backed by each adversary's
overwhelming force
and so we pray diplomacy will ensure
that the world
will have no further carnage to endure
One step at a time
towards the beginning or the end
of international standards
we value and must defend.

Let Your People Go

Leader of Iraq
lead your people back
back from the slaughter
realise
whose safety and future you
jeopardise
by continuing to violate
Kuwait
and what the United Nations declare
to be just and fair.
It is no disgrace
to show compassion
for the human race.
Be resolute and rethink
lead your people
back from the brink.

United

Great Britain was united
all parties gave their support
for the battle that they
had tried to prevent
which in the end
had to be fought
when this nightmare scene
is over
we should not hesitate
to continue through
democracy
to make Great Britain
great.

Democracy Unshaken

Unhesitantly
united
government and opposition
made it clear
that terrorism would not destroy
with fires of hate
the parliamentary procedures
of this our democratic state
and the nation listened
when in the hour of need
defiantly
the Queen
majestically spoke out
courage and moral standards
are what democracy
is about.

Misinformation

The bulletins continue
right throughout the day
and record events to all concerned
in their specific way
how well were we informed
were these the allied gains
were those the enemy losses
doubt lingers and remains
for the bringer of bad news
is never well received
and so no matter who reports
no-one is deceived.

The Awakening

We are not alone
through the years
the wise and the humane
have sought with vision
to create a way
for men and women
to live
without persecution
and division.
Their dreams
for a while came true
but with each dawn
the reality
for when we from our dreams
awake
our share of disappointments
are there for us to take.

Raising the Standards

No jingoistic cheers
but a determination
despite natural fears
to play their individual part
as protectors of the values
of the united nations
men and women
on land and sea
and in the air
professionals
who prepare to give their lives
if need be
to ensure that Kuwait
will once again be free
and as they battle
let us not forget
the part that we must play
to ensure
that peace when won
will be secure.

A Pinch of Salt

A grain of sand
A pinch of salt
taken
with each report
while we at home
watch and listen
out there in the front
there's no remission
we wish them safely home again
professionals
they remain
their integrity
who can deny
committed
they could not stoop to lie
despite the strain
a grain of sand
a pinch of salt
taken
with each report.

Wholesale Slaughter

The enemy of my enemy
is now our deadly foe
Who has now a crystal ball?
How were we to know?
All that is true
but where we were at fault
is in supplying those lethal weapons
for the enemy's onslaught.
Will we now learn the lesson?
Can sanity prevail?
Or do we have once more to tread
a sordid, sorrowful trail?

Faith and Hope

Unprovoked
the champions of the Holy War
attack innocent people once more
in the Holy Land
and give them in no uncertain way to
understand
'We will make them swim in their own blood'
assisted by the indiscriminate use of
the SCUD
this man whom our Prime Minister
stressed has no pity
reveals his inhumanity
once again by attacking
civilians in Tel Aviv city
can Israel resist their intrinsic need
to retaliate
we here can only pray and wait
hoping that the combined allied might
will defeat the onslaught
and restore to the world an order
that is just and right.

Peace Overtures

The Nobel Prize Winner
for services to Peace
President Gorbachev
continues with his mission
and still he does not cease
from trying with diplomacy
across the great divide
to somehow find a link
but however much he tried
there was no way of being sure
that we could take on trust
the words of Saddam
a man
who continued so ruthlessly
to fire the oil-wells
and scorch the earth to dust.

Sacrificial

Burnt offerings
to the Mother of All Wars
blacken the skies
and below
life dies.

Oil On Troubled Waters

Waging war
with weapons more terrible
than ever before
in the need to speed the end of the
occupation
targets are bombed to saturation
and the blood of the economy
oozes out aimlessly
transforming into a slick
of thick provoking oil
choking life
requiring years of toil
to eradicate its pollution.
Wars can be won
but the peace is lost
if we do not work to find a solution.

No Turning Back

Out in the desert
on course
with their powerful
united force
the Stars and Stripes
and the Union Jack
are determined there will be
no turning back
until the world is sure
there are not the means
for yet another
more deadly war
diplomacy
may yet achieve
what we believe
is a just and lasting peace
and secure a regime of trust
but until Saddam relinquishes
his destructive force
there can be no change of course.

Storm Clouds

The exercise is over
war now rears its bloody head
out in the desert no peace
but the slaughter
we all dread
with the clamour for a Holy War
and the building up of hate
there was no way through diplomacy
to bring freedom to Kuwait
and now the tragic scene is set
and before more lives are lost
let us pray for a speedy victory
without a still higher cost
and with a world of Nations United
find our painful way
to a better understanding
and for the peace when achieved to stay.

A Salute

No war diary
would be complete
without due deference
to the man
who played such a decisive part
in securing
the enemy's defeat
he kept them guessing
we were all taken by surprise
but he carried out
his plan of action
and won the ultimate prize
the man who fought his way
in action
to the top
the irrepressible
irreplaceable
General Schwarzkopf.

The Break of Day

Israel
you have been courageous
and wise
and we all now can visualise
the time when
you look up to the skies
and see no enemy
to fill your nights with fear
the Scuds silenced
withdrawn
and with renewed faith
you can rebuild
and face
a more hopeful dawn.

After the Storm

When the pollution in the seas
and the poisonous clouds disperse
and the air and soil is free
there can be no real victory
to celebrate
if we allow arms manufacturers
to carry on as before
providing the means
for yet another war
now is the time to regulate
for in Dubai November '91
it may be too late.

Through Clenched Teeth

There can be no easy peace
to follow this upheaval
this battle which none of us sought
to eliminate an evil
but before we find
disillusion
when hostilities are brought
at last
to their inevitable conclusion
bear in mind
we cannot expect brotherly love to
reign
but through clenched teeth
will have to build the peace again.

The Food of Love

The orchestra played
sweet music
in tune
whilst the discordant cries
of the chosen people
penetrated
adding another note
that was silenced
by the sickly sweetness
of lethal gas
of their last breaths
and yesterday in Tel Aviv
the Israeli Symphony Orchestra
and violinist
Isaac Stern
played
whilst the screeching Scud intruded
disturbing the harmony
but the children
of holocaust survivors
donning their gas masks
stayed and listened
to their music
protected
at home in the Land of Israel
Allies scanning the skies
reinforced
with undying commitment
to their promised land.

Dialogue

The oil wells smoulder
blackening the sky
a visible menace
a warning
on high
but there is another fuse
which if alight
will erupt to reveal
a more damaging sight
the smouldering emotions
of hostility and hate
which we must learn to understand
and try to abate
or when this war is over
and won
our task will have only just begun
diplomats, politicians
every faith and creed
there must be a dialogue
if we are to succeed.

The Young The Brave and The Strong

Hospitals
at the ready
Medical staff
prepared
back home
everybody cared
and when
contrary to all belief
the injuries were few
we all experienced the relief
until the casualties came through
our grief was not for numbers
our loss was each precious one
someone's daughter, sister, brother
someone's father, husband, son
we shall remember them
those who helped to right a wrong
how could we ever forget
the young the brave the strong.

Reconstruction

We look towards the day
when the united skills
of the world
will help to rebuild
what has been destroyed
in the effort to free
Kuwait
from tyranny
and men and women
of different creeds and place
will together erect new bridges
to unite
the vulnerable human race.

A Universal Committment

When the Allied forces withdraw
with the battle against aggression fought and won,
will the war be over then
for everyone?
or shall we see instead of peace
an agonising struggle
that will not cease
in divided Iraq
and if the world cannot
directly intervene
nor turn its back
on this unfolding tragic scene
will the suffering people there
comprehend
that for them
this is how the war will end?
Where is Humanity's heart
Where is the soul
if silenced citizens are left to flee
left to surrender
or seek sanctuary?
If this then is
beyond our control
how limited and restricted
is our goal?
All wars leave wounds
that we must help to heal
to this end
universally
we must now appeal.